SOUTHERN TURKEY

**Mediterranean Coast
and Cappadocia**

Jack Altman

CONTENTS

This Way Southern Turkey	**3**
Map: West and Central Turkey	4–5
Flashback	**9**
On the Scene	**17**
Turquoise Coast	*17*
Map: Mediterranean Coast	18–19
Fethiye 17, Ölüdeniz 20, Dalyan 21,	
Xanthos 21, Patara 22, Kalkan 23,	
Kaş 23, Kekova 25, Demre 26	
Around Antalya	*29*
Antalya 29, Termessos 30, Kemer 31,	
Phaselis 32, Perge 32, Aspendos 33,	
Side 33, Manavgat 35	
East fron Alanya to Antakya	*37*
Alanya 37, Anamur 39, Silifke 39,	
Uzuncaburç 39, Kızkalesi 40, Tarsus 41,	
Adana 41, Antakya 42	
Cappadocia and Konya	*44*
Map: Cappadocia	45
Nevşehir 44, Üçhisar 44, Göreme 46,	
Ürgüp 47, Avanos 47, Derinkuyu 48,	
Ihlara Valley 48, Sultanhanı 50,	
Konya 50, Eğirdir 51	
Cultural Notes	**52**
Shopping	**55**
Dining Out	**57**
Sports	**59**
The Hard Facts	**60**
Index	64

This Way Southern Turkey

Pleasure Coast

The sunny, modern beach resorts of southern Turkey offer a wealth of hedonistic pleasures, while the classical Greek and Roman monuments along the coast provide serious stimulation for the brain cells. The resorts around Antalya are within easy reach of ancient archaeological sites like Perge and the great theatre of Aspendos. And there are plenty more in the hinterland.

Antalya is the undisputed capital of Turkey's Mediterranean resorts. But fine facilities for water sports—and cheerful nightlife—are also to be found west along the aptly named Turquoise Coast around Fethiye, Kalkan and Kaş or east at Side, Alanya and Kızkalesi. In early spring you can ski in the morning up at the new resort of Saklıkent and then take a refreshing swim at Antalya in the afternoon. And you can take your choice between fine sandy beaches for family bathing, or secluded creeks sheltered by steep cliffs if you're looking for something more romantic.

Those craggy coves are the final slopes of the densely wooded Toros (or Taurus) mountains as they descend to the sea. If you're not averse to a bracing hike, then set off to explore the mountains' pine forests. But the region's star attraction is a tour of Cappadocia's astounding lunar landscapes. Weathered over thousands of years, bizarre pillars of volcanic tuff seem to stand guard over underground villages dug out of the rock. At the western edge of Cappadocia, the mysteries of Islam's whirling dervishes can be examined first-hand in the mosques and museums of the holy city of Konya. See, too, medieval caravanserais where Arab and Turkish merchants stopped on their way between Istanbul, Damascus and Baghdad. Or cool off with some freshwater fishing at the peaceful lake resort of Eğirdir.

Olives, Oranges and Lemons

The area we define as southern Turkey runs from the Aegean coast to the Syrian border. It is part of what geographers refer to as Asia Minor, known since ancient times as Anatolia (which in Greek means, like the Levant, the land where the sun rises). It figured prominently in ancient and medieval history. Alexander the Great marched east along the coast and inland around Cap-

THIS WAY SOUTHERN TURKEY

Soft sell with smiles: sesame-ring vendors in Adana, perhaps on the brink of an entrepreneurial career?

padocia on his way to conquer Persia. Apostle Paul travelled in the other direction to carry his Christian mission to sceptical Jews and more receptive Gentiles. Conquest by Selçuk Turks in the 11th century paved the way for the Ottoman Empire.

The great majority of Turkey's tourists converge on this region, which is a relatively small segment of a country roughly the size of France and Britain together or more than twice the area of Germany.

The countryside is classically Mediterranean—orange and lemon orchards guaranteeing year-round fresh juice, olive groves, plantations of palm trees, bananas and luscious avocados for your shrimp salad. Not forgetting peanuts and sesame seeds. You can expect 300 days of sun a year and real rain only in the months of January and February. Winter is otherwise quite balmy, spring and autumn delightful and summer dazzlingly hot and dry. Cappadocia is at its very best in April and October.

The People

Fiercely patriotic, the Turks are also remarkably self-assured, conscious of their long, rich history. This makes them warm and hospitable hosts, whether in the bazaar, café or restaurant, even more so—if you are fortunate enough to be invited—in their homes. The people are easy-going but certainly not lacking in dignity. However casual your clothing may be for the beach, remember to dress with a certain modesty and be prepared to take your shoes off when visiting a mosque.

Ethnically, the Turks are most proud of their Osmanli—Ottoman—origins from Central Asia, but they are now a complex mixture of peoples that have over the centuries flowed in and out of the country from the far-flung empire in Asia and Mediterranean Europe. Since 1989 and the break-up of the Soviet Union and Yugoslavia, there has been a new influx of Muslims from the Caucasus and the Balkans. Today, some 80 per cent of the population (now around 60 million) are Turks, 17 per cent Kurds. Fully 99 per cent of the national population is Muslim, the rest a sprinkling of Greek Orthodox and Armenian Christians, "Latin" Catholics and Jews of Sephardic (Spanish) origin—mostly in Istanbul and the larger towns on the Aegean.

Sweet Temptations

Traditional Turkish crafts are not neglected, though the temptations of cheap mass production for the tourist market turn out the inevitable mountains of gaudy souvenirs. In the major resorts, you will find high-quality gold and silver jewellery, ceramics modelled after the patterns of mosques and sultan's palaces, silk, as well as woollen carpets and textiles and finely tailored leatherwear and luggage. Courteous bargaining rather than vulgar haggling is the order of the day, sweetened by the persuasive sales-talk of a glass of tea or thick Turkish coffee.

One of the hardest tasks on any trip to Turkey is resisting the sweets—not just the famous Turkish Delight *(loukoum)* in a surprising variety of colours and flavours but also the plethora of pastries dripping with nuts and honey. Perhaps even more than its architecture or other more "prestigious" aspects of its culture, the most enduring legacy of the Ottoman Empire is Turkish cuisine, which has left its mark all around the eastern Mediterranean, the Black Sea and North Africa. At its best, it can be compared with the finest in the world. You can find good examples, beyond the obvious "tourist traps", in some of the more traditional establishments in the bigger resorts—both succulent lamb dishes and delicious fresh seafood. The pleasures of Southern Turkey know no bounds.

Flashback

Beginnings

Stone Age men and women were making a living in Anatolia at least ten thousand years ago. Earliest traces of human activity in the country we now call Turkey —a few fragments of bone, stone weapons and tools—were left in upland caves north of Antalya by hunters and gatherers of fruit and nuts. But by 6500 BC, farming communities were springing up across the Anatolian plateau, living in tight clusters of mudbrick houses on stone foundations, like the village of Çatalhüyük excavated north of present-day Konya. The people produced wall-paintings with the bull's head emblem, brightly polished pottery, and terracotta fertility goddesses, broad-hipped and big-bosomed.

By 3000 BC, the working of copper, bronze and other metals evolved through contacts with Mediterranean islands to the west and the Black Sea peoples of the Caucasus to the north. Clan-ruled kingdoms built fortified settlements. Gold jewellery, musical instruments and more elegantly sculptured earth goddesses found in the royal tombs suggest they enjoyed a certain prosperity.

Merchants from Mesopotamia and Assyria led their caravans across Asia Minor to the Bosphorus, trading their textiles and tin for Cappadocian copper. They appreciated, too, the local Hatti people's decorative pottery. More valuable than the exchange of goods was the commerce in knowledge. Foreign techniques in irrigation were traded for Anatolian know-how in metallurgy.

Cappadocia: the Hittites

The origins of the Hittites are uncertain. They arrived in central Anatolia some time around 1800 BC. Speakers of the earliest known Indo-European language, they came from the north, but scholars have not been able to determine whether they skirted the Black Sea on the west side, from the Balkans, or the east, from the Russian Caucasus. They established their capital at Hattusa (modern Boğazkale) on the northern edge of Cappadocia.

After conquering the Hatti, the Hittites proved lenient and open-minded for their time, notably egalitarian in rights of men and

Carved into the cliffside at Myra, Lycian tombs from the 4th century BC.

women. A king and queen shared the throne, advised by a legislature of freemen—landowners, bureaucrats and craftsmen—while slaves were allowed to marry and maintain private property. The Hittites happily adopted the local gods, creating a pantheon of several hundred deities. The Mesopotamian and Anatolian cultures inspired their intricately worked gold and bronze ornaments, and they adapted the cuneiform and hieroglyphic alphabets of Sumer and Babylon for their extensive libraries. Trade with Syria and Egypt prospered from the Cilician ports of Mersin, Tarsus and Adana.

The Hittites extended their empire into Mesopotamia with campaigns against the Mitanni and Babylonians from the 16th to 14th centuries BC. After emerging undefeated—contrary to subsequent pharaonic propaganda—in the vital battle of Kadesh in 1285 BC, they forced the mighty Egypt of Ramses II to share with them control of the eastern Mediterranean.

The empire crumbled in 1200 BC under successive assaults by Caucasian tribes from the north, Assyrians from the east and mysterious invaders known as the Sea Peoples from the across the Aegean. It was probably as refuges against these attackers that Cappadocia's first underground settlements were created, a network of dwellings and sanctuaries hollowed out from the plateau's volcanic bedrock. As Anatolia plunged into a long Dark Age, the Hittites did at least attract Greek entrepreneurs with their skills in iron-smelting, and Greek art and religion were injected with Oriental elements. The Assyrians had destroyed the last vestiges of Hittite civilization by 700 BC.

Lycia, Pamphylia and Cilicia

Lycia covers an area west of Antalya roughly equivalent to the modern Turquoise Coast and its hinterland. It was created by another Indo-European people who arrived in Anatolia around the same time as the Hittites and shared a similar language and culture. They set up their capital at Xanthos (south of Fethiye) and made a reputation as enterprising sailors and fierce pirates. Their warriors are mentioned in Homer's *Iliad* as valiant allies of the Trojans against the Greeks.

East of Lycia, the Mediterranean regions of Pamphylia and Cilicia were settled, according to tradition, by veterans of the Trojan Wars in the 12th century BC. Pamphylia was a loose confederation covering the area between what are now Antalya and Alanya. Its cities of Perge, Sillyon,

Aspendos and Side prospered individually, but they were constantly exploited as pawns in power struggles between the Persians and stronger neighbours like King Midas's Lydia on the Aegean coast.

Stretching further east to the Syrian border, Cilicia was founded, so it is said, by the legendary sage, Mopsus. He apparently established his supremacy as a great seer by correctly predicting the number of piglets to which a sow was about to give birth and the number of figs to be harvested from one venerable tree—a bushel plus one. Cilicia's capital, Tarsus, and the other ports of Mersin and Adana were made vassals of the Assyrians in the 8th century BC and fell to the Persians 200 years later.

The Persians swept through Cilicia and Pamphylia and went on to conquer Lycia and the Aegean coast in 546 BC. Xanthos fell in a mass suicide after the men set fire to the city, in which they had shut up their women and children, before going off to die to the last man against the overwhelming forces of the Persian general, Harpagus. The Persians controlled directly the Anatolian hinterland and installed the proxy rule of satraps along the coast. Individual cities participated in the revolt of the Ionian League, led by eastern Aegean ports, but they were vanquished and subsequently obliged to contribute ships to the Persians' invasion fleet against Greece in 480 BC.

Alexander Cuts the Knot

The Persians retrenched after their defeat at the hands of the Greeks and loosened their hold on Anatolia. For over a century, the cities of Cappadocia and the southern Mediterranean enjoyed relative autonomy until "liberated" from Persian suzerainty by Alexander the Great's passage through Asia Minor.

The 21-year-old soldier from Macedonia crossed the Dardanelles onto the shores of Anatolia in 334 BC. He seized the Persian satrapies along the Aegean coast and bestowed on each the joys of Greek democracy before turning east into Lycia. His reception

THE BEST CARAVANSERAI Of the medieval fortified hostelries guaranteeing merchants a safe night's rest for man and beast, one of the most impressive is **Sultanhanı**, on the Cappadocia road between Aksaray and Konya.

FLASHBACK

there was mixed. Xanthos was cool to all foreign invaders, but accepted any enemy of the Persians. Phaselis received him with a banquet, a golden crown and guides to show him the way along the coast.

In the hilly hinterland, he had to fight his way around recalcitrant Termessos and Aspendos before marching north to Gordion to join up with other Macedonian forces. Confronting there the famous Gordian knot whose undoing, as legend promised, would lead to the conquest of Asia, he is said to have impatiently sliced it with his sword before heading back south through the mountain pass of the Cilician Gates.

After two months in Tarsus recovering from illness, Alexander defeated the Persian armies of Emperor Darius at Issus near the Syrian frontier. He celebrated by founding the city of Alexandretta (modern Iskenderun) south of the battlefield and went on to fulfil the Gordian omen before dying in Babylon in 323 BC.

Roman Rule

Alexander's successors, the Seleucids and Ptolemies, fought over Anatolia until it passed progressively into the hands of the Romans in the 2nd century BC—except for Lycia, which once more asserted its independence, till AD 43.

The region prospered quietly, as attested by its ancient cities' many splendid temples and theatres, but remained a political backwater. The great lawyer-statesman Cicero regarded his 12 months' governorship of Cilicia, 51–50 BC, as a political humiliation.

A few years later, as part of Mark Antony's eastern Mediterranean domain, Cilicia's ports and its forests, precious for construction timber, were a wedding gift to his beloved Cleopatra.

Hard Times for Apostles

Christianity made a controversial start in Anatolia when the first apostolic church outside Palestine was established by Peter in Antioch (modern Turkish Antakya). The capital of Roman Syria was the empire's third greatest city—after Rome itself and Alexandria—and notorious for its sexual debauchery. It was here that Jesus's disciples were first called Christians as they prepared to spread their master's message.

Among them was Paul, a Cilician Jew of Roman citizenship born in Tarsus. From the year AD 45, he embarked with Barnabas, a tough teacher from Cyprus, on a series of missions through Asia Minor and later around Greece. In Anatolia, they tried preaching at synagogues in Perge, Antioch in Pisidia and Ico-

FLASHBACK

Historical footnote: the mighty emperor Frederick Barbarossa perished during the Third Crusade by drowning in this little river near Silifke.

nium (modern Konya). The Jews stoned them and chased them out of town, and Paul decided thereafter to concentrate on Gentiles.

Byzantines and the First Turks

The 4th-century split-up of Roman power placed Anatolia in the eastern empire of Byzantium, the city on the Bosphorus renamed Constantinople after Emperor Constantine. Formally converted to Christianity only on his deathbed in 337, he respected its moral superiority over Roman paganism but saw in it above all a useful expedient to impose unity on his empire. In the 7th century, as the Byzantine capital bathed in opulent luxury, Christian communities in Cappadocia attacked by Arabs from the east sought refuge in the ancient underground villages.

The Selçuk Turks, nomads from Central Asia, entered the Byzantine realm in the 11th century. Converting to Islam as mercenary soldiers for the Abbasid Arab empire, the Selçuks gradually took over all the territories they conquered in the Middle East. They drove the Byzantines to the western rim of Anatolia and established their capital at Konya in 1099. Trade prospered through a network of caravanserais linking Anatolia with Arabia and Mesopotamia. Konya was a centre of decorative arts and philosophy, promoting orthodox Sunni Islam with impressive mosques and theological colleges, but also providing a haven for the dissident sect of dervishes.

Ottoman Empire

In the 13th century, with Byzantine power shattered by the "help" of rampaging Christian Crusaders from Europe, the Selçuk empire was in turn left in ruins by a wave of Mongol invaders. Anatolia was ripped apart by rival tribes and emirates until a tougher breed of Turks emerged triumphant. Lasting over six centuries, the Osmanli dynasty ("Ottoman" to the western world) was founded by Osman I around 1290. Another Mongol attack, by Tamerlane in 1402, slowed down but could not halt the inexorable advance on Constantinople, which fell in 1453. (Istanbul, as the city was known to the Turks, was a name adopted abroad only in the 20th century.)

The first Ottoman sultans showed more religious tolerance to "infidels" than to non-Sunni Muslims. Italian, French and Greek Christians were invited back to Constantinople, as well as thousands of Jews expelled from Spain in 1492. But Sultan Selim the Grim (1512–20) slaughtered 40,000 Shi'ites in Anatolia to combat the influence of his Islamic rival, the Shah of Persia.

Ottoman glory in overseas conquest and the opulence of palace life brought little joy to the country folk of Anatolia. A corps of headstrong Janissary (Yeniçeri) soldiers, originally converted Christian prisoners of war, took care of internal stability. They had to be kept happy with land grants, often confiscated from Anatolian peasants who gradually deserted the countryside to look for better times in Istanbul—a phenomenon that continues to this day.

Atatürk's Republic

Efforts to halt the decline of the empire with modernization came too late. After a revolt at Salonica (Thessaloniki) in 1908, army officers, lawyers and teachers known as Young Turks overcame conservative opposition to a new parliament and replaced Sultan Abd Al-Hamid with his younger brother Mehmet V. The rebels' political wing, the Committee for Union and Progress (CUP), imposed authoritarian government, and alliance with the losing side in World War I hastened the end of the empire.

Turkey became a republic in 1923, moving its capital inland to Ankara. In the same year, the

Treaty of Lausanne ending the war between Greece and Turkey brought about a massive exchange of populations—and place-names—on the Mediterranean coast.

Mustafa Kemal became Turkey's first president. Better known by his adopted name of Atatürk (Father of the Turks), the brilliant but despotic architect of the new nation had risen to prominence with Turkey's single military triumph of World War I, halting the Allies at Gallipoli in 1915. After defeating the Greeks in the wars of 1919–1922, he headed the Turkish National Assembly which abolished the sultanate.

From 1925 to 1935, Atatürk's drastic reforms force-marched Turkey into the modern age. Agriculture, industry and the legal system were all remodelled on Western lines. Islamic authority was replaced by secular institutions, and the alphabet of the Turkish language changed practically overnight from Arabic to Latin. Women were given the vote in 1934 (12 years before the French), while the traditional fez and turban were banned. Anatolians were amazed to see their leader visit small towns to explain his reforms in person. Yet, at his death in 1938, Atatürk was revered nationwide, but not beloved.

Into the Future

Intimidated by Nazi Germany into World War II neutrality, the modern Turkish state benefited from massive US aid in 1946 and remained solidly anchored to the west in the post-war era. Parliamentary government has alternated with military dictatorship as the country grapples with industrial and agricultural reforms. Ongoing conflict with the Kurdish minority continues in eastern Anatolia.

Most recently, Turkey has been trying to reconcile two goals of its dual Asian and European identity: a strong alliance with the Turkic-speaking republics emerging from the former Soviet Union—Turkmenistan, Kazakhstan, Uzbekistan—and entry to the European Union. After electing in 1993 its first woman prime minister, Tansu Çiller, the country seemed determined to maintain a forward-looking stance, nurturing modern commerce, electronic technology and a dynamic mass tourism industry. But the 1996 electoral success of the Islamicist Refah (Welfare) party made fundamentalist Necmettin Erbakan the head of a fragile coalition of religious and secular forces. He retired in 1997, leaving Tansu Çiller at the helm. Meanwhile, Atatürk's portrait remains in shops and offices as a symbol of the modern age.

On the Scene

Turkey's busiest Mediterranean resorts are concentrated mainly at the western end: the Turquoise Coast around Fethiye and the region between Antalya and Alanya. Things get quieter further east for visitors to St Paul's birthplace at Tarsus and the distinctly Arabian atmosphere around Antakya close to the Syrian border. In the interior, Cappadocia has excellent facilities at Nevşehir, Göreme and Ürgüp, with excursions to the religious centre of Konya and tranquil Lake Eğirdir.

TURQUOISE COAST
Fethiye, Ölüdeniz, Dalyan, Xanthos, Patara, Kalkan, Kaş, Kekova, Demre

The romantically named region coincides roughly with the ancient kingdom of Lycia. Geography favoured its fiercely defended independence with the sheltering natural ramparts of jagged Baba, Ak and Bey peaks at the western end of the pine-clad Taurus mountains.

Long accessible only to a privileged yachting fraternity for cruises in and out of its craggy coves and creeks, the coast now boasts a modern highway linking its airport at Dalaman to Antalya and all points east. The Turquoise Coast as such extends from the Dalyan beach resort just west of the airport to the regional capital, Finike, with the centrally located port of Fethiye as the most convenient base for excursions. Many of the best secluded beaches are still reachable only by sea, but all the resorts provide boat rentals.

Fethiye
This busy market town combines good beaches and other admirable tourist amenities with fascinating vestiges of its ancient past. It is built on the Lycian site of Telmessos. Its rock-cut tombs are immediately visible on the hillside behind the town, and stone sarcophagi from the 4th century BC lie scattered around. (Fethiye was known by its Greek inhabitants as Makri until they were

replaced by Turks in the population exchange of 1923.) Earthquakes in 1856 and 1957 destroyed most of the town's historic buildings, but the bustling bazaar (Çarşi) area tucked away in the narrow streets behind Atatürk Boulevard has lost none of its traditional atmosphere.

Telmessos Necropolis

The Lycians buried their dead in tombs cut from the rock face on the hillside looming as backdrop to the bazaar. Some of the more modest are carved in the form of ancient Lycian dwellings with the stone imitating elements of the wooden structure such as doorposts and roof beams. Others, influenced by the progressive settlement of colonists from Greece, are miniature versions of Greek temples with Ionic-columned porticoes and pediments, all carved from the stone. The best known of these is the Amyntas Tomb, bearing the Greek inscription *Amyntou tou Ermagiou* (Amyntas, son of Hermagios), well worth the climb of 150 steps.

Archaeological Museum

The municipality has assembled here some interesting finds from nearby ancient sites. They include a gold leaf tiara from Pinara (3rd century BC) and, from the sanctuary of Letoön, a stone slab inscribed in three languages. Just as the British Museum's trilingual Rosetta stone permitted the deciphering of Egyptian hieroglyphics, so the text here in Greek, Aramaean and Lycian has enabled scholars to begin unravelling the local language, one of the earliest known examples of

Indo-European. The text pays tribute to Kaunos, divine king of Xanthos, the Lycian capital.

Castle of the Knights of St John

The ruins are popularly traced back to a medieval fortress built by Crusaders, who had their main stronghold on the nearby island of Rhodes. Much of the masonry was clearly recycled from the city's Lycian and Greek era and later used, too, by Byzantine and Turkish forces before earthquakes rather than foreign invaders reduced it to its present state.

Gulf of Fethiye

Some of the best examples of Lycian sarcophagi can be seen scattered along the harbour's quayside promenade. From here you can take boat cruises around the 12 islands in the bay, some of them including opportunities for swimming and picnics in quiet coves. The diving here is particularly good, with the chance of spotting dolphins, turtles and other marine creatures as well as underwater caves and even submerged Byzantine ruins—but don't disturb the antiquities.

Beaches

Among the best are Çaliş, an extended crescent of sand and pebble beach, and Günlükbaşı, 5 km (3 miles) north of town. Both are accessible by road or boat.

Kaya

Just 15 km (9 miles) south of Fethiye, and once known as Levissi, Kaya is now just a ghost town, a poignant legacy of age-old Greco-Turkish hostilities but

19

ÖLÜDENİZ

No yachts are allowed to ruffle the blue waters of Ölüdeniz.

also of an effort to salvage a modicum of mutual respect. Some 2,000 little houses stand abandoned on their hillside since 1923. That was when the Treaty of Lausanne ordered the departure of hundreds of thousands of Greeks whose families had lived for centuries in Istanbul, Izmir or other towns of Anatolia and simultaneously of Turks who had never known any home but Crete or Rhodes or Salonica. Elsewhere, Turkish "immigrants" occupied or rebuilt the Greek houses and transformed churches into mosques. Here, almost all the houses were left untouched. On what was once the main street, the dilapidated 19th-century Greek Orthodox church of Panayia Pirgiotissa preserves its marble altar screen and a mural of Jesus and his apostles over the altar. The Greek-Turkish Friendship Society has formulated plans to convert the town into a site for arts festivals.

Ölüdeniz

This enormously popular resort which features on all the tourist office posters is idyllically situated around a blue lagoon backed by a pine-forested hill. The sheltered waters, once a favoured haven for pirates, are delightfully warm from April to October.

Indeed, Ölüdeniz owes its name, "Dead Sea", to the tranquillity of its lagoon. You may also like to try a couple of beaches outside the lagoon—Kıdırık and Belceğiz.

Dalyan

A half-hour drive from Dalaman airport, the westernmost of Turquoise Coast beach resorts is famous as a nesting and hatching place for loggerhead turtles, from May to October. As a result, Istuzu beach, at the mouth of the Dalyan river, has become a bone of contention between conservationists and the tourist industry. The turtles are often confused by the night-time lighting of hotels and restaurants. After dark, the beach is declared off-limits to protect the baby turtles, threatened by birds of prey on their hazardous birthday race for the safety of the sea. The next day, you can see the tracks in the sand of the lucky ones, particularly in July and August. Take a boat-cruise on the Dalyan river for a view of otherwise inaccessible ancient rock-cut tombs.

Xanthos

The coastal highway No. 400 runs inland east of Fethiye to the town of Kınık, 64 km (40 miles) away, from which it is a 20-minute walk to Xanthos, the ancient hilltop capital of Lycia. For its historic interest and the beauty of its position high above the lovely valley of the Eşen river, the archaeological site is one of the most impressive in southern Anatolia. Over the centuries, it suffered three disasters. Facing attack by the Persians in 546 BC and again by Brutus, Julius Caesar's assassin, in 42 BC, the citizens set fire to their homes and committed collective suicide rather than surrender. Nearly 19 centuries later, there was nobody left to stop the British traveller Charles Fellows from plundering the site of its antiquities and carrying them off to London's British Museum.

At the entrance, a monumental gate from the Hellenistic era is coupled with the Arch of Vespasian (1st century AD). A uniquely Lycian structure in the Mediterranean world of classical antiquity is the remarkable series of pillar-tombs—vaulted sarcophagi mounted on columns—from the 4th century BC and earlier. Some of the sculpted reliefs from the temples and tombs are copies of those pilfered by the British. On the so-called Obelisk Tomb, a lengthy inscription in the Lycian language is still being deciphered. A Greek verse describes exploits of the deceased as warrior and wrestler.

The theatre is Roman and on the hill behind it, the Lycian

XANTHOS • PATARA

acropolis includes a square structure believed to be the royal palace burned down during the Persian invasion. Other structures include rock-cut tombs imitating in stone the Lycians' wooden houses, a Byzantine basilica with mosaic paving and a Byzantine monastery.

Letoön

Before Xanthos, on a side-road west of the coastal highway, is Lycia's national religious sanctuary—and a Christian shrine in the 4th century AD until destroyed by the Arabs 300 years later. Under Lycians and Greeks, three temples were dedicated to the Titan goddess Leto and her children Apollo and Artemis.

Besides remains of the temples, you can see a nymphaeum with a large semi-circular paved pond whose waters are now the home of terrapins and raucously croaking frogs. The latter may be the descendants of herdsmen transformed into frogs by Leto when they drove her away from a drinking fountain on her first visit here. Built over the rectangular part of the nymphaeum, only the foundations of the Christian church can still be discerned.

Patara

Also known by its Turkish name of Gelemiş, the ancient port and modern beach resort due south of Xanthos is above all famous as the birthplace of Santa Claus. The 4th-century St Nicholas became Bishop of Myra, east along the coast at what is now Demre. When you squeeze them, some of the Santa Claus dolls in the souvenir shops say "Ho, ho, ho!" in Turkish. The ancient site has a stately triple-arched entrance (1st century AD) and equally well-preserved Roman theatre from the 2nd century, partially smothered in sand.

MY SON THE MUSICIAN

Taking her name from the Lycian Lada, meaning simply "woman", the goddess Leto was a daughter of Titans and not to be trifled with. A rival of hers, Niobe, proud mother of seven sons and seven daughters, complained of all the fuss made over Leto, who had only two children—even if they were Apollo and Artemis and their father was Zeus. For Niobe's taste, Apollo was too much of a cissy for liking music, and it wasn't very ladylike of Artemis to run around hunting. She forgot they were both pretty good with a bow and arrow. Leto sent her kids to deal with Niobe's. Apollo and Artemis killed six apiece, leaving Niobe with one boy and one girl, just like Leto.

Ripples in the sand at Patara, the biggest and best beach along this coast.

The amazing white sandy beach stretches either side of the river-mouth for a total length of 15 km (9 miles). Part of it is a turtle-nesting beach protected by conservationists, i.e. out of bounds to humans after dark. With high surf waves in July and August, the best family bathing may be in spring and autumn.

Kalkan

Originally a Greek village named Kalamaki, this rather chic resort is a favourite both with yachtsmen using the marina and with ramblers, who go hiking in the splendid woodlands of the Taurus mountains. They all meet up in the harbourfront's first-class restaurants, bars and nightclubs. There is a small but popular pebble beach east of town at Kaputaş.

Kaş

Morning is the time to enjoy the pristine tranquillity of the ancient port's gently curving bay set against dramatic cliffs, with sarcophagi half-concealed in the olive groves. Antiphellos of old, Andifli till 1923, the town has kept its old attractively balconied Greek houses. Kaş is now a boisterous resort with a colourful mixture of foreigners and Turkish bourgeoisie from Istanbul.

Uzunçarşı

The shops, bars and restaurants of the "Long Bazaar" stay open till very late. This is the prime place on the Turquoise Coast for purchasing gold and silver jewellery, ceramics, fine carpets and other craftware.

Ancient Antiphellos

Remains of the ancient port city are scattered around town. At the east end of the Uzunçarşı bazaar, the double-chambered Lycian Lion Tomb is a monumental affair with lion's heads on the vaulted lid of the sarcophagus. Up the hill on Yenı Yol you can see some rock-cut tombs.

On the west side of the city centre are the ruins of a Hellenistic temple and a theatre with 26 rows of seats, where the modern town sometimes stages wrestling matches.

Beaches

The only alternatives to the hotels' swimming pools are the aptly named Büyük Çakıl (Large Gravelly) and Küçük Çakıl (Small Gravelly) beaches east of town, or the pebbles of Kaputaş to the west, shared with the neighbouring resort of Kalkan.

Take a boat from Üçağiz to see the sunken sarcophagus of ancient Simena.

Kekova

Some 30 km (18 miles) east of Kaş, the offshore island of Kekova lies opposite the port of Üçağiz. On a boat trip around its shores and in the inlet separating it from the coast you can see some of Turkey's most enchantingly located ruins: stairways, street-paving, pillars, remains of house walls, stone sarcophagi of anonymous Lycian settlements, all submerged in the shallows. (If you are not staying in Üçağiz itself, boat-cruises are available from Kaş or the port of Andriake,

---

BUSY SANTA

The image of St Nicholas as a gift-toting Father Christmas is a creation of the West. The Eastern Orthodox church honours him as a patron saint for bringing back to life three little boys chopped up and pickled in salt by a butcher—among other miracles. The legend of his generosity tells how Nicholas gave three bags of gold to a poor man unable to provide a dowry for his three daughters, thus saving them from prostitution. A later version transformed the bags into three gold balls and Nicholas became the patron saint of pawnbrokers—as well as virgins, sailors, scholars, merchants and, of course, children.

near Demre to the east.) For those excursions that give you time on Kekova itself, the island has a delightful sandy beach. And quite apart from the rare joy of seeing the ruins sunk beneath the waves, this stretch of creeks and coves along the Turquoise Coast is startlingly beautiful.

Demre (Kale)

Demre, called Kale on the maps, is the modern Turkish town that has grown out of the venerable city of Myra of which Santa Claus, that is to say St Nicholas, was bishop in the 4th century. Besides visiting the bishop's church in the city centre, it is worth seeing the remains of the ancient Lycian site on the northern outskirts, and its nearby port of Andriake, now a starting-point for sightseeing cruises to the sunken ruins off the island of Kekova.

Church of St Nicholas

The first church built on Müze Caddesi was an early Christian edifice of the 3rd century, preceding Nicholas's appointment as bishop. It was rebuilt in 1043 to shelter his tomb, and subsequent miracles prompted his sanctification and attracted hordes of pilgrims. The church has since undergone extensive renovation, notably by the bishop's namesake, Tsar Nicholas I, who erected a belfry and replaced the nave's cupola with a vaulted ceiling in 1862. Turkish architects added the more characteristic Byzantine domes over the narthex (vestibule). The mosaics inside the narthex depict Jesus with Mary and John the Baptist.

A sarcophagus to the left of the church entrance is identified as the tomb of St Nicholas, despite its carving of a married couple. The grave was located beneath paving near the altar; Italian sailors and three priests stole the bones from it in 1087 and took them to Bari's Basilica San Nicola to cash in on the lucrative pilgrim business. Tradition relates Myra to the Greek word for myrrh, a fragrance said to have befuddled the robbers when they

---

2 THE TWO BEST BAZAARS The Turquoise Coast resort of **Kaş** offers a fine choice of carpets, jewellery and ceramics in its famous Uzunçarşı "Long Bazaar". For an intriguing change of atmosphere—more Arabic than Turkish—try the **Antakya** bazaar around Kemal Paşa Caddesi.

DEMRE

Close-up inspection of reliefs embellishing the cliff tombs of Myra.

opened up the tomb. More authentic is the impressive 11th-century Byzantine bishop's throne standing in the apse.

Ancient Myra
The remains of the Lycian city are prettily located on a rocky hillside just north of Demre. The centrepiece is a Greco-Roman theatre built against a cliff. Its huge orchestra is littered with stone carvings from the proscenium décor, including two theatre masks. In the cliffs is a remarkable series of rock-cut tombs. Carved reliefs in the burial chambers depict scenes of battle and funerary processions.

Andriake
Myra's ancient port—also identified now as Çayağzi—is 5 km (3 miles) west of Demre. As a vital outlet for supplying corn to Rome and the empire, it stored the harvest in Hadrian's Granary (2nd century AD), just south of the Androkos river. The massive outer walls still stand as an enclosure for eight storage rooms, with stone busts of the emperor and his wife Sabina over the main gate. Andriake's major attraction is the charming beach of sand dunes running down from the cliffs. Some of the harbour's more friendly fishermen take passengers who want to try their luck.

AROUND ANTALYA

Antalya, Termessos, Kemer, Phaselis, Perge, Aspendos, Side, Manavgat

Antalya is the capital of Turkey's most popular tourist region. Outside Antalya, the Taurus mountains, less rugged here than further east or west, slope gently down to long stretches of sandy beach, ideal for family bathing.

The Greeks named the region Pamphylia, "land of all tribes", following traditional accounts that it was settled at the end of the 12th century BC by the many peoples whose soldiers had participated in the Trojan Wars. It earns its name again in the modern vacation season when all the tribes of northern Europe join others from the Mediterranean. They come to enjoy the water sports around Kemer, Antalya (for its sailing) and Side, and to explore, handily nearby, the excavated cities of Phaselis, Perge and Aspendos.

Antalya

The country's most successful resort seems unstoppable. The metropolitan population is hovering around a million and still growing. The charm of its old town, built on a limestone plateau over the harbour, is enhanced by a delightful climate—mellow year-round except for the searingly hot months of July and August. Ultramodern hotels offer every facility for water sports and other leisure pursuits. Nightlife bounces till dawn. And its location amid some of the Mediterranean coast's most important ancient sites has enabled Antalya to create an archaeological museum ranking only after those of Istanbul and Ankara. The town was founded with the name Attaleia by King Attalus II of Pergamum in the 2nd century BC.

Old Town

Start at the rose-tinted fluted minaret, Yivli Minare, built in the 13th century by the Selçuk sultan Ala'eddin Keykubad. Its adjacent mosque and mausoleum, of a later date, stand on the foundations of a Byzantine church. The fluting is a characteristic feature of Selçuk architecture.

On the eastern edge of the old town, Kaleiçi, the monumental Hadrian's Gate has a triple-arched marble entrance flanked by massive square battlemented towers. It was erected for the emperor's entry into the town in AD 130. Remains of the harbour walls protecting the citadel are Hellenistic and Roman at their base, reinforced with medieval additions by the city's Byzantine,

Selçuk and Crusader occupants. At the south end of the ramparts, Hıdırlık Kulesi watchtower is of Roman origin. It now looks down on the pleasant tea gardens of Karaali Park, shaded by palm trees and other sub-tropical vegetation.

A few elegant if sometimes dilapidated—though progressively renovated—Ottoman houses line the narrow streets of the bazaar area running down to the harbour. Monuments here include the "Broken Minaret" (Kesik Minare) of a mosque damaged by fire. The harbour itself is lined with popular cafés humming with life from early evening, as visitors and townspeople mingle for the daily promenade along the waterfront. The luxurious yachts are moored out on the modern marina along the jetty west of the old harbour.

Archaeological Museum

At the western outskirts of town on the Konyaaltı highway to Kemer, the museum handsomely displays its treasures with clear, multilingual explanations. In the prehistoric section, Stone Age cooking utensils and other implements retrieved from the Karain caves north of Antalya are the earliest traces of human life in Turkey, over 10,000 years old. Finely modelled figurines in ivory and silver in distinctive central Anatolian Phrygian style date from the 7th century BC. Besides some attractive mosaics from the Hellenistic Seleucid period and Byzantine icons from Xanthos, the richest collection of statuary and sculpted stone sarcophagi come from nearby Perge in its Roman era, some of the best devoted to the exploits of Hercules. In the ongoing contest between Turkey and Italy for the genuine remains of Santa Claus, the museum displays a reliquary said to contain some bones of Saint Nicholas, Bishop of Myra.

Beaches

The most popular beaches are gravel Konyaaltı, 3 km (2 miles) west of town, and fine-sand Lara, 12 km (7 miles) east of Antalya. Near Lara, the Düden stream meets the Mediterranean at the Düden Falls.

Termessos

Combine a visit to this ancient site 34 km (21 miles) northwest of Antalya with a bracing walk around the rugged Mount Güllük national park.

The formidable citadel was built on a terrace-like plateau 1,050 m (3,450 ft) up the mountain. It distinguished itself in 333 BC by dissuading Alexander the Great's army, forcing him to make a diversion inland to join reinforcements in the north. From

TERMESSOS • KEMER

At Termessos it's difficult to distinguish the work of Nature from the work of man.

the Roman era, the Royal Road was the main highway into town, past massive defensive walls to solid greystone buildings—the gymnasium with bath houses for the athletes, the agora (marketplace) and monumental mausoleum. The great theatre shows off the full drama of the city's mountain site, with seats for 4,200 spectators. On the other side of the agora, the odeon doubled as a smaller theatre and open-air parliament.

Of the nearby temples, four in all, the most impressive has six Corinthian columns still standing. The necropolis is just a jumble of scores of shattered sarcophagi.

Saklıkent

At this winter sports resort 50 km (31 miles) inland from Antalya, you can ski on the slopes of Mount Bakırlı at altitudes varying between 2,000 m (6,562 ft) and 2,400 m (7,875 ft); they provide perfect conditions both for downhill and cross-country skiing in March and April.

Kemer

This is a fast-growing beach resort with well-equipped holiday villages and superb marina. It also serves as a good base for exploring nearby archaeological sites or rambles in the Olimpos Beydağları national park.

Phaselis

Three natural harbours around a long tree-shaded promontory make this one of the most attractive ancient sites on the Mediterranean coast. Today's visitors can take a swim where Greek and Roman ships loaded construction timber and farm produce for Alexandria 2,000 years ago. Olive trees and shrubs have overgrown its marble paved streets, gateways, jetties and quays. Most romantic of all is a theatre for 1,500 spectators where Greek tragedy alternated with gladiator contests involving wild beasts.

Perge

Remains of this important Pamphylian trading centre are situated 18 km (11 miles) northeast of Antalya—strategically sheltered from marauding pirates but accessible now to tour buses. Greek and Turkish scholars dispute its foundation. While both agree that Trojan war veterans may have settled the area, the Greeks attribute the town's actual creation to other Greek colonists around 1000 BC, and Turks suggest a settlement 500 years earlier by Hittites. Perge, as in Pergamum on the Aegean coast, is an Indo-European Hittite word meaning "high place", referring to the acropolis of its original foundation on a hill at the north end of the excavated site.

The ancient sports and entertainment complex is on the southwest corner of the city, near the tour entrance. A splendid horseshoe-shaped stadium seated 12,000 spectators for its chariot and foot races. The biggest in Asia Minor, it measures 234 m (767 ft) by 34 m (111 ft). Between the arches and pillars of its grandstands, the ancients built shops, taverns and other concessions. Across the road is the theatre. Make your way to the top

THE THREE BEST WALKS The Anatolian countryside is green and varied, and the cool of the forest is often a welcome change from the beach or shadeless archaeological sites. At **Termessos**, a short drive into the mountains from Antalya, you can visit the ancient citadel with a ramble through Mount Güllük national park. South of **Eğirdir**, combine a hike through Kovada Gölü park with some fishing in its lake. Behind **Kalkan**, the Taurus mountains offer a popular change of pace to visiting yachtsmen.

of the 14,000-seat auditorium—42 rows of seats—for a fine view over the ancient city.

The site reveals several layers of building—Seleucid Greek ramparts, Hellenistic and Roman city gates, Roman baths and Byzantine basilica. The main street stretches from the square agora, with a rainwater gutter running down the centre and what were colonnades of shops on either side.

Aspendos

Just 20 km (12 miles) east of Perge, the Pamphylian town boasts one of Anatolia's most superb ancient theatres, certainly the best preserved—thanks to its being used and renovated by Selçuk Turks as a medieval caravanserai. (Its turquoise ceramic tiling is displayed in the Antalya museum.) Built in AD 180 by the great Roman architect Zeno, the stage backdrop rises in two lofty storeys above the Köprü river valley. Rectangular doorways provided five stage entrances. The hemispheric auditorium for 15,000 spectators rises steeply in two tiers of 19 and then 20 rows of seating to an arcaded gallery at the top. It is used for modern arts festivals.

Take a look, too, at the acropolis on the hill above the theatre, with remains of a small temple, nyphaeum and basilica. Striding across the plain to the north is a series of imposing two-tiered arches of the Roman aqueduct that once extended 15 km (9 miles) from the mountain streams to the city.

Side

Unique among Pamphylia's archaeological sites, the old port city of Side is fully integrated into the 20th-century town. Its buildings, hotels, shops, banks, post office and government offices have been erected along streets previously used by the town's Greek, Roman and early Byzantine inhabitants. Sand has silted up the historic harbour, but it has also provided two fine beaches, on either side of the rocky peninsula on which the town is built—74 km (46 miles) from Antalya.

Side means in ancient Anatolian dialect "pomegranate", a symbol found on hoards of coins from its heyday as a trading port. Founded in the 7th century BC by Ionian Greek settlers, it thrived on its rake-off from the vigorous slave trade conducted by Cilician pirates on the marketplace. Roman conquest diminished without ending the trade, but the town declined under Byzantine control and was destroyed by the Arabs in the 7th century AD. It was completely abandoned until the early 1900s when Muslim émigrés arrived from Crete to build

SIDE

Sustenance at hand in Side's Temple of Apollo.

a fishing village—Selimiye—among the ruins. They are the grandparents of many of today's hoteliers, shopkeepers and restaurant-owners. The fishing tradition has been maintained at least in the abundance of seafood restaurants.

Ancient City

The modern highway enters Side through the original main city gate, with a nearby nymphaeum fountain (2nd century AD) that was fed by the Roman aqueduct. The turreted ramparts were built in the Byzantine era. From the gate, two paved colonnaded streets lead into the ancient city, the shorter one due south to ruins of a Byzantine basilica and bishop's palace, half-hidden in the sand dunes. The other, longer main street runs southwest down the middle of the promontory to the square agora where the slave market was held. On the opposite side of the road are the Roman public baths, transformed to house a museum of Side's sculptures, notably of Hercules and Hermes, and sarcophagi with carved reliefs of Eros. Many of the statues were decapitated by early Christian iconoclasts.

Immediately to the south of the museum, Emperor Vespasian's triumphal arch and fountains (1st century AD) lead into the modern town—and the entrance to the great theatre. The biggest in Pamphylia, it enjoys a spectacular location overlooking the two bays on either side of the promontory. Unlike other theatres in the region, the free-standing edifice is built on an infrastructure of arches and vaults once sheltering shops and living quarters for gladiators and wild beasts.

The colonnaded street continued towards the temples of Athena and Apollo, to the end of the promontory and the old harbour. The port was always notorious for the constant dredging needed to keep it clear of silt, a chore as proverbial in the region as the cleaning of the Augean stables.

Beaches

The fine sands flanking Side's promontory stretch for some 10 km (6 miles), lined with water sports clubs and veritable fleets of windsurf boards and small sailcraft for hire. If these beaches become too crowded, try the quieter Kumköy on the far side of the western beach or Sorgun to the east.

Manavgat

This is a popular excursion from Side (and Alanya) for lunch at restaurants on the river or boat-cruises inland to take tea beside the modest but picturesque waterfalls.

Selçuk Caravanserais

East of Manavgat, in the mountains north of the Alanya road, are two 13th-century caravanserais—hostelries that served merchants as way stations between the Selçuk capital, Konya, and the trading port of Alanya. Alarahan was built by Sultan Ala'eddin Keykubad, also responsible for Antalya's Fluted Minaret and Alanya Castle. The other hostelry, Şarapsa Hanı, has been turned into a nightclub.

---

4 THE FOUR BEST ARCHAEOLOGICAL SITES The remains of Anatolia's ancient cities benefit from magnificent natural settings. The Greco-Roman port city of **Phaselis** boasts three harbours on its green and pleasant promontory south of Kemer. Near Antalya, the horseshoe-shaped stadium at **Perge** and superb theatre at **Aspendos** are without their equal in Asia Minor. The distinctive quality of **Side** is the way its ancient monuments are integrated in the modern town.

EAST FROM ALANYA TO ANTAKYA
Alanya, Anamur, Silifke, Uzuncaburç, Kızkalesi, Tarsus, Adana, Antakya

The region stretching from Alanya to the Syrian border encompasses the ancient province of Cilicia. It was infamous in ancient times, even well into the Middle Ages, as a haven for pirates, who sold off their captives as slaves. They took refuge in rocky coves and creeks along the western coast—known as Cilicia Tracheia ("Rough") as opposed to Cilicia Pedias ("Smooth"), the fertile plain further east. The timber of its inland forests were a valued asset for Cleopatra's shipbuilding interests when Mark Antony gave her Cilicia as one of his wedding gifts. The coves, accessible only by boat, still offer escape from the long but often crowded sandy beaches.

Alanya

The town's landmark castle looms on the horizon of its rocky promontory, rising beyond long green banana plantations. As a tourist centre, this is a true boom-town, with modern resort complexes mushrooming along the beaches that extend either side of the promontory. But the place

Ancient and modern knit together nicely at Alanya.

also has a strong characteristic Turkish atmosphere, derived from both the citadel's Selçuk and Ottoman monuments and houses and the traditional restaurants and cafés. This, along with the mild winter, makes it particularly pleasant out of season, too, when the Turks recapture their town from the visitors.

The Byzantines called the promontory Kalonoros, "beautiful mountain". In 1221, its Selçuk conqueror Ala'eddin Keykubad renamed it after himself, Ala'iya, and Atatürk, as part of his reforms, replaced the glottal Arabic sound in the middle with a more European "n"—Alanya.

Harbour

The old Selçuk and Ottoman harbour is on the east side of the promontory, making a delightful promenade among the seafood restaurants and old monuments. It is dominated by the massive Kızıl Kule (Red Tower), 35 m (115 ft) high, built by Ala'eddin Keykubad in 1226 as kingpin of the harbour's defences against perennial attacks from pirates. Today housing a small folklore museum, the octagonal redbrick tower still seems to protect the old wooden houses hugging the slope above.

Further along the waterfront are the Tersane, the workshops of the Selçuk shipyard, and a smaller tower, Tophane, that served as an arsenal.

Castle and Citadel

Sprawling across the "beautiful mountain", the ramparts of Alanya Castle enclose in a citadel what was the whole medieval and Ottoman town. Beyond the main gate, with its Persian inscription, is the self-contained village of Ehmediye with Ottoman houses, a derelict 16th-century mosque and an older Selçuk mausoleum. Past a lighthouse (1720), the winding road ends at the castle proper, İç Kale (inner fortress), together with an abandoned Byzantine church across from the old bazaar. The view from the highest point, 260 m (853 ft) above sea level, looks out west along the Mediterranean and inland north to the Ak Dağ range in the Taurus mountains.

Alanya Museum

Across the street from the Tourist Information Office, in the modern part of town, is a collection of local archaeological finds. The museum also presents a typical Ottoman domestic interior, with fine furnishings and carved wood ceiling and shutters. Take a look, too, at the pleasant garden, once an Ottoman graveyard.

Dim Çayı

One of Alanya's more delightful attractions is the chance to dine while dabbling your feet in the refreshing waters of the Dim Çayı river. Just 6 km (4 miles) east of the city centre, the riverside restaurants set up their tables in the shallows. The people who enjoy it most are those that walked all the way.

Beaches and Caves

Sandy beaches stretch for miles along the coast on either side of the old town, many taken over by hotels and beach clubs. The crowds dwindle as you approach Incekum (Fine Sand) beach at Avsallar, to the west.

As its name gently understates, Damlataş (Cave of Dripping Stones) has some impressive stalagmites and stalactites. (It is signposted close to Alanya Museum.) Cleopatra's Beach—one of many attributed to her along the Cilician coast—can be reached from here on foot. Other caves, among the rocks on the western end of the promontory, are best visited on a boat cruise—Aşıklar (Lovers' Cave), Fosforlu (Phosphorescent Cave) and Korsanlar (Pirates' Cave).

Road to Tarsus

The coast east of Alanya is appreciated mainly for its isolated beaches, secluded coves or the occasional stretch of fine sand, with a backdrop of dense pine forests for rambles into the interior.

Gazipaşa
This unruffled little town has fresh seafood, a pleasant beach and the disparate ruins of ancient Selinus.

Anamur
The town offers a handsome castle, a charming little harbour (Iskele) for waterfront dining and good beach hotels. Some 6 km (4 miles) to the west is the ancient Roman site of Anamurium with remains of an impressive two-storey bath house, assembly hall, theatre and vaulted houses. Outside the walls are an aqueduct, necropolis and the empty shells of three Byzantine chapels.

Silifke
Founded in the 3rd century BC by Seleucus I Nicator, a general of Alexander the Great, this was one of many cities to be named after him, Seleucia. As antiquities, the sleepy modern town boasts only the remnant of a temple of Jupiter (2nd century AD), the Roman bridge over its Göksu Nehri (Blue Waters) river, and a hilltop Byzantine castle—worth the climb for the view. With the road approaching the Syrian border, the cuisine here has more Arabian spice to it.

Uzuncaburç
The 45-minute drive north from Silifke passes grandiose countryside through a rugged gorge in the Taurus mountains, with glimpses amid the olive trees of Roman temple-like tombs, single

---

5 THE FIVE BEST CHRISTIAN SITES As the first region chosen by the apostles to spread the word of Jesus, Anatolia had some of the earliest Christian communities outside Palestine. **Myra**, modern Demre, is famous as the 4th-century bishopric of St Nicholas, attracting hundreds of pilgrims to the church of his tomb. St Peter is believed to have preached around AD 50 in the grotto church bearing his name in **Antakya**. Three outstanding sites in Cappadocia are the underground city of 7th-century Christian refugees at **Derinkuyu**, the valley museum of medieval rock-cut churches at **Göreme**, and the cliffsides of the **Ihlara Valley**, riddled with rock-cut dwellings and churches.

Floating offshore, the fairytale castle of Kızkalesi.

and double-storeyed. Uzuncaburç takes its name—High Tower—from the 22-m (72-ft) structure that was part of the fortifications for the excavated Greek city of Olba. Known to the Romans as Diocaesarea, it stands on the site of an earlier Hittite settlement, but all the remains are Greco-Roman. The theatre is Roman, as is the monumental five-columned gateway leading into the ancient city.

Built in the 3rd century BC, the Hellenistic Temple of Zeus Olbios was one of the first temples to use the florid Corinthian order for its capitals—four remain here on the 30 surviving columns. The Roman system of water supply still feeds the modern city of Uzuncaburç.

Kızkalesi

This agreeable little resort, 25 km (15 miles) east of Silifke, thrives on its seafood restaurants, good hotels, decent beach and fanciful legends surrounding its two castles. The name, meaning Maiden's Castle, refers to the 13th-century pile out on the island, 200 m (220 yd) from the shore. An Armenian king is said to have put his daughter out there to protect her from a prophesied lethal snakebite. But the snake turned up in any case, hidden in a basket of fruit sent by a well-meaning servant—and did its stuff. The castle on land is a more sturdy ruin, interesting mainly for its use of ancient masonry with Greek inscriptions on the main entrance and a complete Roman gate built into the west wall.

Tarsus

Little remains to commemorate its ancient fame as place of the first meeting of Antony and Cleopatra, leading to their romantic and political alliance, and as birthplace of the apostle Paul. Signposts guide pilgrims to St Paul's Well, a water source still functioning in the garden of the house where he is said to have been born. The 16th-century mosque, Ulu Cami, stands on the site of St Paul's cathedral. A Roman gate has been named Cleopatra's Gate—in Turkish, Kancık Kapısı (Gate of the Bitch). The Queen of Egypt sailed into town on the Tarsus—then Cydnus—river in 41 BC. As Shakespeare describes it:

"The barge she sat in,
    like a burnished throne,
Burned on the water:
    the poop was beaten gold;
Purple the sails, and so
    perfumed that
The winds were love-sick
    with them."

(*Antony and Cleopatra*, Act 2, scene 2).

In those days, a lagoon, now silted up, made Tarsus one of Asia Minor's most important trading ports. Paul, born Saul, son of a tent-maker, was justly proud of the ancient city now buried beneath the modern town—"I am a Jew of Tarsus, a city in Cilicia, a citizen of no mean city." Its scholars were renowned throughout the ancient world, most notably the Stoic philosopher Athenodorus.

Adana

With a population well over a million, Turkey's fourth-largest town (after Istanbul, Ankara and Izmir) is a resolutely modern

---

CILICIAN GATES

Travellers between Tarsus and Cappadocia pass by the historic Cilician Gates. An older road retraces the route of Persian emperors, Alexander the Great, and later French Crusader Baudouin in 1097, on his way to becoming King of Jerusalem. The "Gates" are a narrow pass hollowed in the mountains by the Tarsus river, even now barely 20 m (65 ft) wide between rockfaces towering 100 m (328 ft) on either side, in ancient times impregnable against any army commanding the heights.

ADANA • ANTAKYA

place since it was rebuilt by a French colonial administration after World War I. It thrives on a textile industry that draws much of its raw material from surrounding cotton plantations. Across the Seyhan river, the 14-arch Roman bridge built by Emperor Hadrian is rare testimony to the city's ancient origins—it was a constant bone of contention between Persians and the Greeks and Romans. The Archaeological Museum contains some fine prehistoric ceramics, a few Hittite artefacts and some Hellenistic and Roman sculpture. The Syrian-style white and black marble Ulu Cami was built in 1507 by Emir Halil Bey, whose tomb there is decorated with mosaics and ceramic tiles.

The Road to Antakya

The Mediterranean coast turns south at Dörtyol, close to the battlefield of Issus, where Alexander the Great won a decisive victory over Persia's king Darius III in 333 BC. (Centuries of earthquakes have made it impossible to identify the exact spot.) Nearby Iskenderun is the nondescript industrial centre and port built over Alexandretta, the first of the Macedonian conqueror's many commemorative cities.

The Hatay region, of which Antakya is capital, is an Arab enclave given to Syria after World War I. The French handed it over to Turkey in 1939 and it has been a frequent object of dispute.

Antakya

The atmosphere of the town (often signposted as Hatay) is distinctly Arabic, in cuisine, architecture and the relaxed pace of life. A strong Christian minority reminds us that for the apostle Peter, ancient Antioch was the most important Christian community outside Jerusalem. As capital of Roman Syria, it rivalled Rome and Alexandria in luxury and sin. The Archaeological Museum illustrates the fact with a collection of startlingly well-preserved mosaics from Roman villas. They depict, beside the usual heroics of mythology, some eye-opening scenes of opulence and debauchery. In the more sedate and virtuous modern town, there is considerable colour in the bazaar around Kemal Paşa Caddesi north of the ancient Rana Köprüsü Bridge. On the northern outskirts of town is St Peter's grotto church (Sen Piyer Kilisesi), where the apostle is believed to have preached around the year AD 50. The 12th-century façade was added by Crusaders.

Harvesting peanuts in the Anamur hinterland.

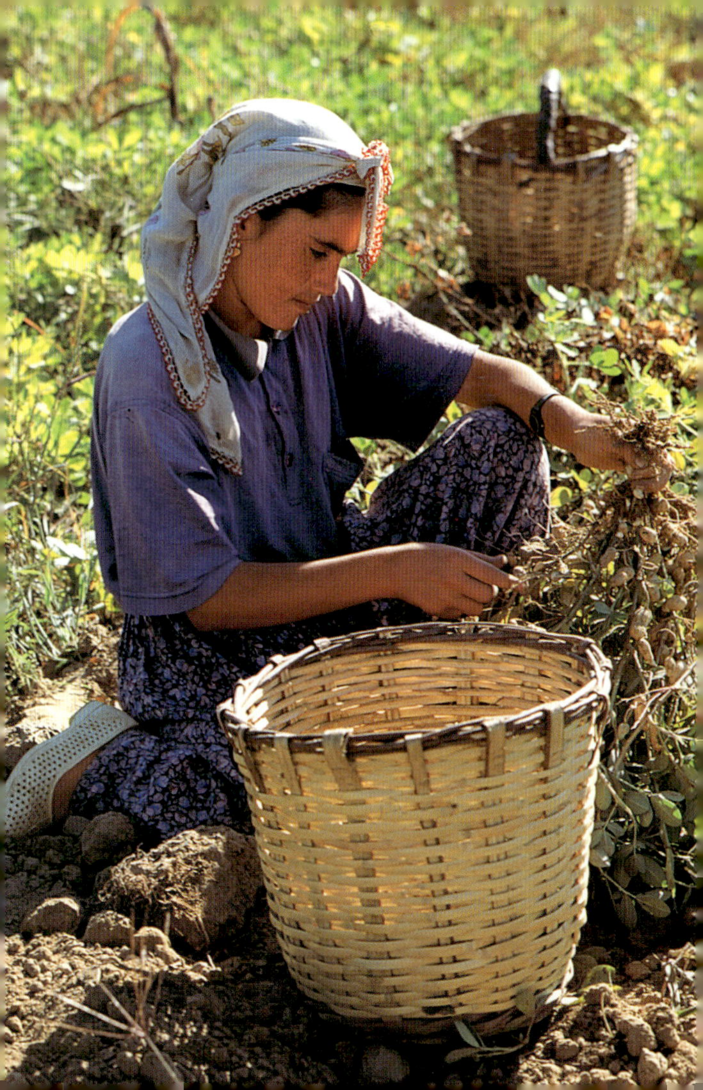

CAPPADOCIA AND KONYA

Nevşehir, Üçhisar, Göreme, Ürgüp, Avanos, Derinkuyu, Ihlara Valley, Sultanhanı, Konya, Eğirdir

The eerie landscape at the centre of the Anatolian plateau is the source of dreams for a lifetime. No other place on earth is quite like it. Over eons of time, nature has created a unique topography that man has in turn transformed for his needs, both practical and spiritual. Dubbed by the Turks "fairy chimneys", armies of slender pinnacles surround white hillocks hollowed out by man into still inhabited dwellings, plunging canyons where the russet rockfaces have been sculpted into churches. In flatter areas, invisible to the casual passer-by, whole underground cities spread their network of homes and sanctuaries beneath your feet.

The volcanoes at the origin of this phenomenon deposited a fertile soil that has enriched the region. Per capita, Cappadocia is the wealthiest province in Turkey. The wines are good and the farm produce excellent, as are the local crafts—textiles, gold, silver and above all the ceramics for which the same basic techniques and fine red clay have been used since the Hittites settled here nearly 4,000 years ago.

Cappadocia, from the ancient Persian Katpatukya, means "land of beautiful horses", and its thoroughbreds are still highly esteemed today—available for hire, too.

Nevşehir

The tourist boom has merely added to Nevşehir's long-standing prosperity as a market town. Colourful characters from all over Cappadocia flock to the Eski Sanay market from Sunday morning to Monday night. What remains of the hilltop Selçuk citadel is interesting mainly as a vantage point to view the surrounding countryside. On the way up, take a look at the 18th-century mosque of Damat Ibrahim Paşa, the town's most famous son, Grand Vizier to Sultan Ahmet III. In the museum on Yeni Kayseri, collections trace the region's history from Roman to Ottoman times, with particularly fine kilims, carpets and jewellery.

Üçhisar

Just 3 km (2 miles) east of Nevşehir, the stone outcrop rising 60 m (196 ft) above the modern village affords a first glimpse of Cappadocia's cave dwellings carved out of the rockface. They are no longer inhabited but open for visitors, and the view from the top is worth the climb.

CAPPADOCIA
Gülşehir
Açıksaray
Kızılırmak
Avanos
Sarıhıdır
Sulusaray
Çökek
Çat
Ulaşlı
Çavuşin
Zelve
Göreme
Kizilçukur
Ürgüp
Nar
Üçhisar
NEVŞEHIR
Ortahisar
Ibrahimpaşa
Göre
Mustafapaşa
Kavak
Acıgöl
Güvercinlik
Bahçeli
Çardak
Ayvalı
Güneyce
Cemilköy
Kızılcın
Taşkınpaşa
Mazıköy
Kaymaklı
Sahinefendi
Özlüce
Tilköy
Çakıllı
N
Başköy
KEY
Fairy Chimneys
Underground City
Derinkuyu
Güzelöz
0 2 4 6 8 10 km
0 3 6 miles

Göreme

The town's valley of rock-cut churches, 10 km (6 miles) east of Nevşehir, is one of the main attractions of any visit to Cappadocia. Local onyx factories produce and sell carved jewellery and ornaments.

Göreme Valley Museum

Dozens of 10th- and 11th-century rock-cut churches can be seen on a walk through this magic landscape of pinnacles, hillocks, cones and sheer cliffs. Medievalists have located in this sprawling monastic sanctuary more than 300 places of worship. The visitors' paths are modern additions for what is now an open-air museum.

The 10th-century Tokalı Kilise (Church of the Buckle) can claim the most beautifully preserved frescoes, painted against a brilliant blue background—the long-gone buckle was a gold ring in the ceiling. In the apse and over the altar, the Passion, Crucifixion, Entombment and Resurrection of Jesus are depicted with solemn elegance.

Even without a structural purpose, columns, arches, barrel-vaults and domes have been intricately sculpted from the volcanic tuff to respect the design of classical Byzantine architecture. The best examples of these, all 11th-century, are Çarıklı (Church of the Sandals), Karanlık (Dark Church), notable for the detail of its façade, and Elmalı (Church of the Apple). In each of them, the Greek-cross plan is crowned by a central dome depicting Jesus Pantocrator ("All Powerful") reigning over the Archangels. Other churches, more austerely decorated, represent the conventional themes with a simple cross, fish or other ritual symbol.

NATURE'S SOFTWARE AND HARDWARE

The creation of Cappadocia's natural marvels began millions of years ago when ash from volcanic eruption spilled across the plateau and compacted into a thick layer of soft volcanic tuff. The eruptions scattered thinner patches of hard basalt lava on top, which was gradually fissured by time and the elements. Rainwater seeped into deepening cracks and eroded away the porous tuff below into separate hillocks, still topped by the solid stratum of basalt. Hillocks weathered down to mounds and then slender pillars, each balancing a crown of basalt—the "fairy chimneys". In areas without this protective hard crust, wind and rain gouged out spectacular canyons like Ihlara Valley.

Glorious blue frescoes in the Church of the Buckle (Tokalı).

Ürgüp

This lively, entertaining resort is a charming Anatolian town that has preserved many handsome Greek and Ottoman houses, largely 19th-century. Looming over the town are cliffs dotted with old cave dwellings that now serve as storerooms, warehouses and donkey stables. Market gardens, vineyards and apple orchards line the banks of the Damsa river. In shops on Cumhuriyet Square and along Kayseri Caddesi, you will find first-class ceramics, gold and silver jewellery, carpets, kilims and antiquities from eastern Anatolia. At the town's wineries, taste the local production—the best are the whites. Many of the better bars and nightclubs offer authentic Turkish music, both traditional and modern.

Avanos

The hillside town, Vanessa to the Romans, is famous for its red pottery made from the clay of the fast-flowing Kızılırmak, "Red River". Known in ancient times as the Halys, this is the longest river in Asia Minor, rising in Central Anatolia and curving in a wide loop of some 1,150 km (715 miles) past Avanos and north to the Black Sea. Visit the potters' workshops in vaulted cellars, where techniques and materials remain essentially unchanged since the great heyday of the Hittites. Hand-knitted sweaters are another Avanos speciality. And Cappadocia's time-honoured reputation for its horses can be tested at the town's stables, which organize treks in the surrounding countryside.

Derinkuyu

About 30 km (18 miles) south of Nevşehir, this is one of the most remarkable of the mysterious underground cities. In its present form, you will see the bedrooms, kitchens, storage rooms, wine press and church of a Christian community that sought refuge from Arab attackers, probably in the 7th century. Derinkuyu ("Deep Well") may, however, be the elaboration of considerably older settlements, indicated by the discovery of Roman tombs and what might be a Hittite flour mill. So far, seven levels of the underground city have been excavated, to a depth of over 90 m (300 ft), with the upper two levels open to the public. There is good electric lighting and the original ventilation of vertical air shafts still works very well. (Claustrophobes should avoid the narrower passages.) The city spread out in an amazing network of passages to cover fully 4 sq km (1½ sq miles), potentially accommodating up to 20,000 people. Huge stone wheels could be rolled to block passages from invaders and labyrinthine escape routes are thought to have extended at least 9 km (5 miles) north of Derinkuyu.

Ihlara Valley

This plunging canyon on the region's southern periphery, 70 km (43 miles) from Nevşehir, provides perhaps the most dramatic setting of all the rock-cut dwellings and churches in Cappadocia. The sanctuaries are set in stark, red cliffs in sharp contrast to the serene valley floor of junipers, green shrubbery and wild grapevines. The valley was occupied by the Peristrema monastic community from the 9th to the 14th century, though there is evidence that the first churches hewn from the rockface date back to the 6th century.

A plan at the southern entrance indicates the most accessible churches. Kokar Church, literally "fragrant" though the reason why seems to have disappeared, depicts in its vaulted nave New Testament scenes from the Annunciation to the Last Supper. A hand painted in the dome sym-

Three-hatted chimneys pixilate the landscape near Zelve.

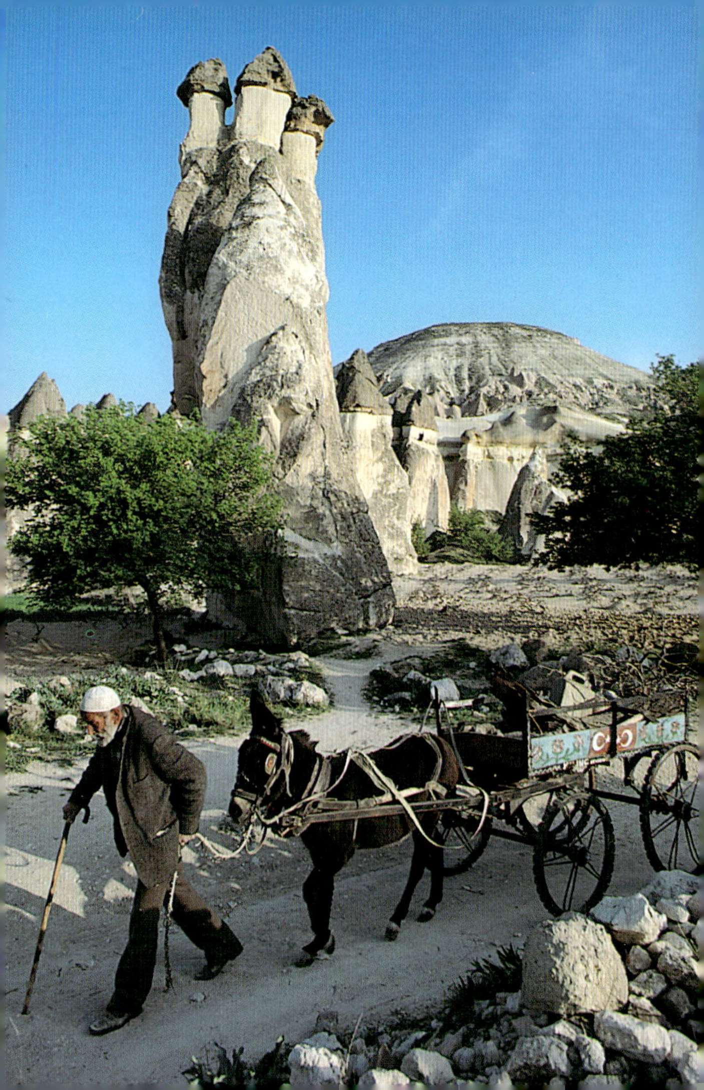

bolizes the Trinity. The cross-shaped Ağaçaltı Church (Beneath the Tree) is dedicated to Daniel, shown with his lions in the western transept. A fine fresco of the Adoration of the Magi has a distinctly eastern, possibly Iranian style. Best known is Yılanlı, the Church of the Snakes, depicting the Day of Judgement with women in hell being bitten by serpents for their sins. Satan is portrayed as a snake with three heads.

Aksaray

The market town northwest of the valley provides a convenient base for the visit and for the onward journey to Konya. Take a look at Ulu Cami, a mosque founded in the 13th century with a handsome Selçuk pulpit *(mimber)*, and the Kadıroğlu theological seminary, also Selçuk but rebuilt in the 16th century.

Sultanhanı

The Cappadocia circuit heading back to the coast via Konya, the region's ancient capital and home of the Whirling Dervishes, crosses a fertile plain of wheat fields. As did merchants of old, it passes through the Selçuk caravanserai of Sultanhanı.

Looming out of the plain some 50 km (30 miles) west of Aksaray, Sultanhanı looks more like a massive fortress than a hostelry for tired merchants and their camels. But that is just what was needed in the violent days of brigandry in the 13th century. Centred in the lofty limestone outer wall, the gatehouse is a veritable castle keep, with a splendid ornate arch framing an intricately carved pendentive above the doorway. In the inner courtyard is a mosque raised on a platform of four pillars—to keep out any wandering mules or camels. They were coddled, fed and bedded in the vast monumental hall opposite the gatehouse, in five vaulted aisles of stalls. Flanking the entrance are the merchants' spacious quarters and bath-houses, simpler dormitories for servants, plus smithy, carpentry shops and cellars.

Konya

The old Selçuk capital is revered by devout Muslims as the historic centre of the Mevlevi, Sufic mystics known to the West as Whirling Dervishes. Far from being rabid zealots, the dervishes practise a highly tolerant, undogmatic creed that prizes poetic beauty, love and generosity. Their places of worship and study and the mausoleum of their 13th-century founder, Afghan-born Mevlana Celaleddin Rumi, have been preserved as an impressive museum attracting pilgrims from all over the Islamic world.

Mevlana Museum

The 13th-century turquoise-domed sanctuary of the dervishes houses the tomb of the Mevlana ("our leader") in a compound that includes the dervishes' cells, their library and the hall in which they performed their whirling dance. Atatürk transformed the compound into a museum in 1927, but it retains the sanctity of a holy place; visitors are asked to remove their shoes, and to dress with the modesty required of a mosque. The devout gather at the iron grill protecting the master's intricately carved sarcophagus. His family and disciples are entombed nearby, along with traditional costumes, prayer carpets and an early illuminated text of Mevlana's Persian-language poetic masterpiece, the *Mathnawi*.

Next door, the 16th-century Semahane hall is the circular room in which the ritual dance called the *sema* was performed. It now exhibits the dervishes' musical instruments, including the distinctive reed flute or *ney*, 13th-century kilims and carpets, and exquisitely wrought prayer-hall lamps. Another room displays ancient illuminated Korans and a casket said to contain hairs from the Prophet Mohammed's beard.

A demonstration of the whirling dervishes' dance is performed in Konya during the week preceding the anniversary of the Mevlana's death, December 17, in a converted sports arena.

Other Islamic Buildings

The Karatay Medresesi, a 13th-century Selçuk theological seminary, has been transformed into a ceramics museum, but it is worth visiting for its own architecture. The main portal unites ornate Islamic design with Corinthian columns recycled from a Roman temple, which frame a finely carved classical Selçuk pendentive archway. The skill of Selçuk craftsmen is visible again in the ceramics adorning the interior's Dome of Stars and the bird and animal motifs in the galleries. Another superb Selçuk portal can be seen at the Ince Minare (Slender Minaret) seminary. The best of the mosques is the Ala'eddin Camii, which also makes abundant use of ancient Roman columns.

Eğirdir

This appealing lakeside resort, 234 km (145 miles) west of Konya, has attractive features for an overnight stay—a boat-cruise on the lake; a trip north to the Roman ruins of Antioch ad Pisidium; and, 35 km (21 miles) south, a walk in the delightful woods of the Kovada Gölü national park, with good fishing in its lake.

CULTURAL NOTES

Atatürk. Literally "Father of the Turks", the name was adopted by the nation's revered Mustafa Kemal in 1934 when ordering all citizens to use a surname rather than traditional combinations of son's and father's first names. As part of his Westernization programme, Atatürk (1881–1938) personally conducted lessons in public parks in how to use the Latin rather than Arabic alphabet. He also set an example in modern dress, replacing his old fez with a black European homburg.

Caravanserai. More than just an inn or hostelry, the "caravan-palace" (*kervansaray* in Turkish), where Arab and Turkish merchants stopped to eat, sleep and water their camels, mules and horses, was a veritable fortified hamlet. Inside its walls were a mosque for prayer, sleeping accommodation—more or less spacious according to the status of master or servant—and courtyards where they met to exchange information and merchandise. As an ongoing investment in the merchants' custom, accommodation and services at the caravanserai were paid by the sultan for the first three days.

Coffeehouses. Practically out of bounds to women, the most lively *kahvehane* are around or right inside the bazaar. Today, tea rather than coffee is served, strong and sugared in tulip glasses. The men play dominoes, introduced to Istanbul by Venetian merchants, or backgammon *(tavla)*, which originated in ancient Babylon and Egypt. Customers puff away at a *narghile* of compressed Persian tobacco, lit by embers of charcoal, with the smoke cooled through a long lamb's-leather tube. For a more "Western" allure, some prefer the yellowish clay-like meerschaum pipe.

Hamam. The Turkish bath has separate hours for men *(erkekler)* and women *(kadınlar)*. Bathers are given wooden clogs and a cotton wrap for wandering around the hamam, and a proper towel for drying later. After a steam bath in a marble-walled room comes a climactic massage on a heated stone slab. The pummelling and pressing can be followed by an equally vigorous "peeling" of dried skin with an abrasive glove.

Kilim. This subtly patterned flat woven rug, without pile, is the oldest of all Turkish carpets. It is depicted on murals in the Stone Age village of Çatalhüyük (6500 BC). Its motifs and colours have age-old symbols. Red: goodness and wealth; blue: nobility; green: paradise; yellow and black: against the evil eye.

Underground Cities. The phenomenon of whole communities in Cappadocia seeking refuge from invaders underground was first recorded by a Greek soldier, Xenophon, when he retreated through Asia Minor in 401 BC at the head of an army of mercenaries hired by the Persian king Cyrus. In his account of the retreat, he noted: "The houses were built underground, reached by an entrance like the mouth of an unusual well that widened the deeper it went. For the animals, sloping tunnels were dug out of the earth, with stairways for men. In the houses were sheep, goats, cows, chickens and other livestock with their young. There was dry grass for the animals, and great jars for storing oil, wheat and barley wine. The thirsty could use long hollow reeds of various lengths for sipping the wine from the jars. This barley wine was very strong and was best watered down."

Whirling Dervishes. Poetry, music and dance, contrary to Islamic orthodoxy, are central to the faith of the Mevlevi dervishes. For the whirling dance, the *sema,* gesture and costume combine with the music to evoke its unique purpose: ritual communion with God. Serenely reconciled with the notion of death, the dervishes cast aside a black cape symbolizing the tomb to dance barefoot in a long white tunic (the shroud), and a camelhair turban (the tomb's headstone). The music is celestial and the dancers turn like the heavenly spheres. The right arm extends upward to receive God's grace and the left arm down to pass it on immediately to mankind. Musicians chant mystic hymns as the dancers whirl into an hours-long trance.

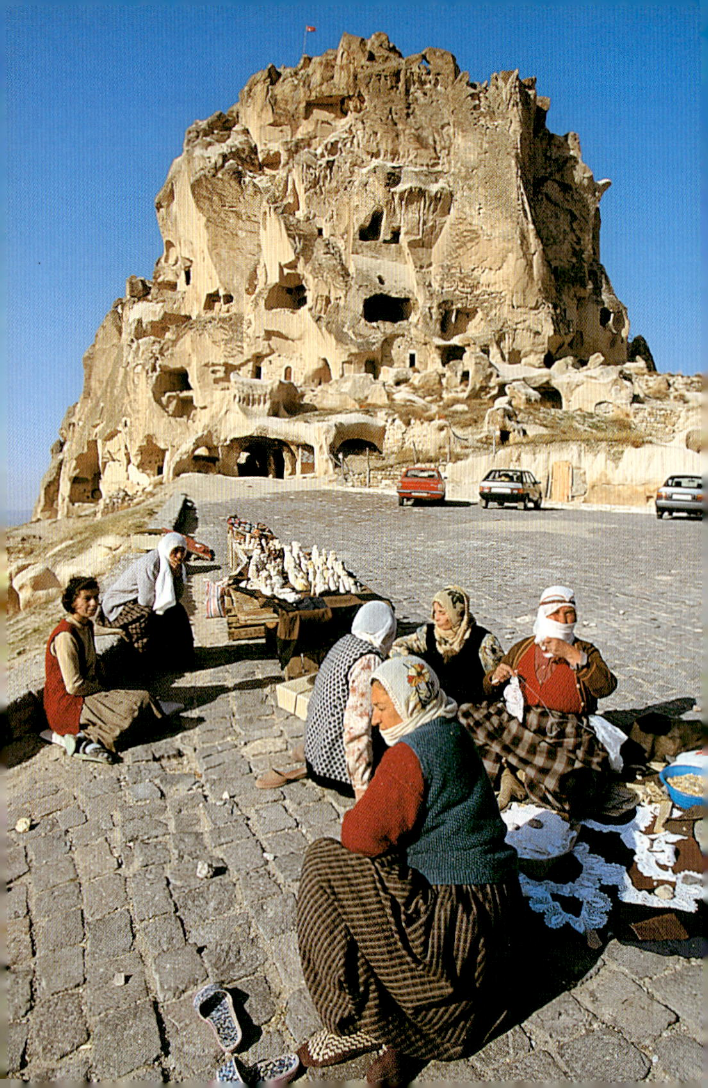

Shopping

For Turks, the marketplace is the centre of social intercourse. It's the place to meet, have a shoe-shine, haircut or shave, drink a glass of tea. There is less hard sell than you might imagine. Like the offer of tea or coffee, bargaining is as much a social ritual as commercial obligation. But of course that inevitable: "Where are you from?" is not just a friendly first question, it's an opening gambit in gauging the sales prospect and appropriate technique. They don't treat a British customer as they would an American or charm the French with the same approach as to the Germans.

Where?
Almost every town of any size has its bazaar area. Even if there is no covered *bedesten* set aside for the purpose, the same time-honoured "folklore" applies. Major resorts like Antalya and Alanya sell their leather, carpets and jewellery in "high street" shops. High-quality merchandise from eastern Anatolia comes to prosperous Cappadocia before going on to Istanbul, with the best selection in Ürgüp.

What?
To buy things that capture the real atmosphere of Turkey, it's a good idea not to shop before you've gained a feeling for the place. On the practical side, make sure they are not too big or too fragile to pack.

Antiques
It is illegal to export antiquities of artistic or archaeological value, including old carpets, but other antiques such as Ottoman samovars, ornaments, glassware, *narghile* hookah pipes, even old jewellery are allowed. When in doubt, ask an official before purchasing. For the best antique silver, try the shops at Kaş on the Turquoise Coast or Cappadocia's Ürgüp. Around ancient Greco-Roman sites, ignore vendors of old coins or statuary; these are either fake or illegal.

Carpets and Kilims
Used as floor or wall-coverings, Turkish carpets are justly renowned for their brilliant patterns and workmanship. The most expensive are of pure silk, but

you may prefer fine-tufted wool for everyday use. Unlike knotted carpets, kilims are flat woven without pile. When choosing your pattern, you may not mind if the motifs symbolize good fortune, piety, love or fertility, but check on the colour dye by discreetly rubbing with a damp white cloth. If it stains the cloth, the colour is artificial.

Ceramics

Visitors to Cappadocia should seek out Avanos red clay pottery, made just the way the Hittites did it 4,000 years ago, though you will also find more modern styles besides the traditional ware. Look out for the brilliantly coloured tiles like those that used to decorate the sultans' palaces and mosques. They are still a great buy, along with plates, bowls and jugs for which cerulean blue is the most valued colour.

Fashion

Turkey's modern fashion designers have burst on the international scene with subtle combinations of western and traditional Turkish styles using Bursa silk and the Ankara region's angora wool. You will find much the same selection in boutiques in Antalya, Alanya and Ürgüp as you might in Istanbul. Among peasant clothes, light cotton blouses and headscarves are popular and the brightly coloured heavy woollen socks are great for winter. Beside the solid cowhide bags, look for the finest Anatolian lambskin leathers used for coats, jackets and lighter garments. Avanos in Cappadocia produces fine knitted sweaters.

Copper and Brassware

Best buys are hand-crafted samovars, pots and cups for Turkish coffee, lamps and candlesticks. Copper cooking utensils such as tea-kettles should be lined with tin.

Jewellery

Cappadocian onyx is used both for ornaments and jewellery, but the cheapest and most popular jewel is the ceramic or glass blue bead to ward off the Evil Eye. Among other semi-precious stones, amber and turquoise are the most prized. Gold and silver jewellery is sold by weight, leaving the quality and design of workmanship, particularly eastern Anatolian filigreed silver, to your personal taste.

Musical Instruments

Of Turkey's traditional instruments, easiest to carry home are the *davul* drum, the *ney* (Dervish flute) and the *saz*, a long-necked lute. For the authentic product steer clear of souvenir shops. Your best bet is Konya.

Dining Out

The Ottoman Empire spread its cuisine throughout the Mediterranean, so that much of what you find today in Greece, Egypt, Lebanon and further afield in North Africa is of Turkish origin. For lovers of meat or fish or vegetarians, it is rich and varied and by no means limited to the all-too-familiar kebabs. Turks are natural hedonists and enjoy their food as much for its colour, texture and aroma as for its sheer nourishment. So besides the usual hotel meals, try to get out to the town restaurants and share the appetizing Turkish experience.

To Start With...

The famous appetizers, *meze*, can in fact make a whole meal, so just have a taste of each if you want a main course, too. Cold delicacies, eaten with white bread or unleavened *pide* (Turkish pita-bread): aubergine (eggplant) mashed with lemon (*patlıcan salatası*) or sautéed slices (*patlıcan kızartması*); chopped tomato, cucumber and green salad (*çoban salatası*); stuffed bell-peppers, cabbage or vine-leaves with rice, pine nuts and minced meat (*dolma*); dips of salty tarama fish roe paste, tangy *tahina* sesame-seed or cool garlicky yoghurt and chopped cucumber (*cacik*). Warm starters include fried mussels (*midye tavası*); light pastry stuffed with cheese or meat (*böregi*); and thin-sliced mutton liver (*arnavut ciğeri*).

Main Course

Coastal fisheries offer a fine range of fresh seafood: red mullet (*barbunya*), swordfish (*kılıç*), bass (*levrek*), bream (*saragöz*), prawns (*karides*), squid (*kalamar*) and mussels (*midye*). These are best lightly fried or charcoal-grilled. Chips (French fries) will be served if you insist, but the Turks prefer a little salad.

You'll find kebabs galore, lamb, mutton or beef: familiar *şiş kebap* with tomato, green pepper and onion, spiced-up *adana kebap*, ever-popular *döner kebap* sliced from its vertical skewer and its rich Bursa variation, *Iskender kebap* drenched in a yoghurt sauce. Turkish gourmets recommend stuffed leg of lamb (*kuzu dolması*) or the hearty *güveç*, a spicy meat and vegetable stew cooked in a clay pot. Try

DINING OUT

köfte meatballs or barbecued *kokoreç* mutton tripe. Roast chickens *(piliç)* are generally small but tasty.

Vegetarians should go for the great vegetable stew *(türlü sebze)*. Besides the ubiquitous aubergine, there are all manner of bean dishes: a solid white bean-soup *(kuru fasulye)*, green beans in tomato sauce *(zeytinyağlı fasulye)* and broad beans *(bakla)*. Look out, too, for okra *(bamya)*, spinach *(ispanak)* and cauliflower *(karnabahar)*. But remember: these dishes may in any case be cooked in a meat stock.

Desserts

Turkish sweetmeats are an enduring monument to the wonderful self-indulgence of the Ottoman Empire, a world power that drowned in a sea of nuts and fruit dripping with honey and rose syrup—smiling. The best known pastries are *baklava* filled with marzipan, honey and pistachios; *kadayıf*, like shredded wheat baked with sesame, almonds and honey. Besides rose syrup, Turkish Delight *(loukoum)* is made with hazelnut or pistachio, as is the *helva* sesame paste. *Sütlaç* rice pudding is more delicious than anything you had at school. Ice cream *(dondurma)* is high-quality, too. And two delicacies from the harem: "lady's navel" *(hanım göbeği)*, a kind of creamy doughnut; and "beloved's lips" *(diber dudağı)*, almonds, walnuts, honey and rose syrup.

Drinks

The most nervous travellers can be reassured by the ready availability of mineral water—with bubbles *(maden suyu)* or without *(memba suyu)*. The beer is good, the national Efes Pilsen or locally produced Tuborg. The aniseed-flavoured apéritif, *rakı*, customarily accompanies *meze* and is drunk diluted with water and ice or straight, with water (or beer) on the side. Turkish wines *(şarap)* have been produced in Cappadocia, western Anatolia and Thrace since earliest antiquity, drunk in moderate quantities but uninhibited by the strictures of Islam. White wines *(beyaz)* are probably best in quality, particularly with seafood, but the reds *(kırmızı)* and rosé *(roze)* are quite respectable. Slightly alcoholized grape juice *(şıra)* is also popular, as are non-alcoholic fruit juices *(meyva suyu)*—freshly squeezed orange or grapefruit.

Turkish coffee *(kahve)* is now more popular with discerning foreigners than with the Turks themselves. Ask for the strong thick brew sweet *(çok şekerli)*, medium *(orta şekerli)* or without sugar *(sade)*. The Turks prefer tea *(çay)*, served strong in small tulip glasses, without milk.

Sport

Beyond the obvious (and limitless) choice of water sports on the Mediterranean coast, it is worth considering the dry-land sporting possibilities of the national parks in the Taurus mountains. Or take a leaf out of the book of those Hittites and try horseback riding in Cappadocia.

Water Sports

Antalya, Kaş, Ölüdeniz and Alanya all have superb facilities for sailing, windsurfing, snorkelling, water-skiing and paragliding. Scuba diving among the underwater archaeological sites off Kekova Island needs official authorization. The marinas at these resorts offer day-trip cruises to remoter coves for swimmers seeking a little tranquillity away from the family beaches, in addition to longer cruises on yachts, chartered with or without a crew. Spartan swimmers welcome the challenge of the chill lake and river waters around Eğirdir.

Fishing

You don't need a licence to go line or net fishing off the beach. At Andriake and Patara, friendly fishermen may take you out for an early morning's deep-sea fishing. The catch includes sea bass, red mullet, mackerel, spiny lobster, crab and shrimp. Try freshwater fishing—carp, bass, trout and crayfish—in the lakes of Eğirdir and nearby Kovada Gölü.

Tennis

Big hotels at the major Mediterranean resorts have hard courts, floodlit at night, often the most comfortable time to play.

Horseback Riding

The best place to hire horses in Cappadocia is at Avanos, which has a stable of about 20 locally bred animals.

Hiking and Skiing

For hiking in the national parks, try Güllük Dağ (near Termessos, west of Antalya) or the Köprülü Valley park north of Aspendos. In the interior lake district, the Kova Gölü park is conveniently close to Eğirdir. At Antalya's ski resort, Saklıkent, the slopes of Mount Bakırlı provide opportunities for downhill and cross-country skiing in March and April.

The Hard Facts

To help you plan your trip, here are some of the practical details you should know about Southern Turkey.

Airports
International and charter flights fly via Istanbul to Dalaman for the Turquoise Coast, directly to Antalya for other Mediterranean resorts, and to Konya or Kayseri for Cappadocia. The airports provide banking, car-hire and tourist information office services, in addition to duty-free shop, restaurant and snack bar facilities.

Climate
Spring and autumn are pleasant. Summers are hot and sticky, with temperatures reaching the high 20s C (mid-80s F) on the coast. Average noon temperatures from April to June rise in Antalya from 17° to 23°C (63°–75°F), in Cappadocia from 12° to 20°C (54°–68°F). In the autumn, they range around 23°C (75°F) in Antalya, 19°C (66°F) in Cappadocia. Winters are mild around Antalya and Alanya but generally rainy and cool in the interior.

Communications
Your holiday postcards may take a long time to reach home unless you disguise them by putting them inside envelopes. Post them in the slot marked *Yurtdişi* (overseas). The post office is marked PTT and the stamps counter indicated by the sign *pul*.

Turkey is progressively installing a modern telecommunication system for fax and phone. You can call worldwide with phonecards *(telekart)* from streetphones, much cheaper than the hotel's surcharge service. To make an international call, dial 00, then the country code (1 for US and Canada, 44 for UK), the area code minus the initial zero, and the local number.

Crime
Southern Turkey poses no problem for personal security and people are predominantly honest. Pickpockets—very often a fellow tourist—may be a problem in the bazaars, street markets or crowded public transport. Without being paranoid, don't tempt them with an open handbag or a wallet in the hip pocket. Put valuables in the hotel safe. Drug offences are severely punished by long prison sentences.

Driving
Before deciding to rent a car, you should know that Turkish drivers are frenetically impatient and have one of the highest accident rates in the Mediterranean region. Driving in the bigger towns is more hassle than it's worth. In any case, be sure you have a valid national licence or International Driving Permit. Rental age limit is over 21. To avoid unpleasant surprises, check on the exact extent of varying insurance coverages, personal, fire, collision, theft, etc. Drive on the right, overtake on the left, drive defensively but not at a snail's pace.

Electric Current
All appliances need double round-pin plugs for 220 volts AC, 50 Hz.

Emergencies
Most problems can be handled at your hotel desk. Telephone number for police: **155**, ambulance **112**, fire brigade **110**. Consular help is there only for critical situations, lost passports or worse, not for lost cash or plane tickets.

Essentials
You won't need much formal wear. Pack a sun-hat and add a sweater for cool evenings. Good walking shoes are vital, especially for archaeological sites and Cappadocia, and easy-to-kick-off sandals or moccasins for the mosques—headscarves for women. Include insect repellent and a pocket torch (flashlight) for the rock-cut churches and underground cities in Cappadocia.

Formalities
Citizens of most countries need only a valid passport, but British, Irish and American citizens must purchase a visa at point of entry (about £10, $20).

Customs controls are minimal at point of entry, with an official import allowance, duty-free, of 200 cigarettes and 50 cigars or 200 g tobacco, 5 litres of wine or spirits. No limit on import of foreign currency, though amounts should be declared on arrival and noted in your passport. Important valuables like expensive jewels or electronic equipment may also be noted on a form accompanying your passport to avoid difficulties on departure. The purchase and export of antiquities are prohibited.

Health
Apart from minor stomach upsets from change of diet, the big health hazard in Turkey is the sun. Watch out for sunstroke, heat exhaustion and dehydration. Stick to the shade, wear a hat, use a good sun-screen, drink plenty of water, it's as simple as that. To be on the safe side, stick to bot-

The Hard Facts

tled mineral water. For emergencies, make sure your health insurance covers holiday illnesses as Turkey's social security does not extend to foreign visitors. Doctors, dentists and hospital staff in large towns are well trained, many speaking good English or German. If you expect to need prescription medicines, take your own as you may not find the exact equivalent on the spot. In an emergency, you'll find good antidiarrhoea pills at the pharmacy *(eczane)*. Along the coast, protect yourself against mosquitoes.

Language

English and German have gradually replaced French as the Turks' second language. Except for hotels or other tourist establishments, do not expect to find anything but Turkish spoken outside the major resorts.

Media

Most European newspapers and European editions of American dailies are available, a day or so late, in major resorts. International affairs and Turkish politics are covered in the *Turkish Daily News*, published in English. Many major hotels have satellite dishes for BBC World Service, Sky News or CNN television. BBC and Voice of America radio are all accessible on short wave. Turkish state radio and TV also have English, French and German language news programmes.

Money

The national unit of currency is the Turkish lira, in denominations so high that you often have to calculate in millions. Coins from 500 to 5,000 lira. Banknotes from 5,000 to 500,000 lira.

Many major shops and restaurants in the resorts welcome credit cards, as well as Eurocheques and traveller's cheques. Smaller establishments prefer cash.

Opening hours

The following times are given as a general guide, some of them subject to variations.

Banks open 8.30 a.m.–noon and 1.30–5.30 p.m. in tourist areas.

Shops are open non-stop from around 8 or 8.30 a.m. to 7 or 8 p.m., later in some bazaars. Sunday is the usual closing day, but by no means compulsory everywhere.

Main post offices open from 8.30 a.m. to 12.30 p.m. and 1.30 to 5.30 p.m.

Museums, archaeological sites and palaces usually close on Mondays only.

Photography

Film for video or still-cameras is of course readily available in

Turkey. Choose film-speeds for the brilliant Mediterranean light. Most museums, palaces and archaeological sites allow cameras, but usually for an extra fee, with restrictions on the use of flash. Avoid photographing Muslims at prayer. For other equally obvious reasons, avoid photographing areas involving military security —airports, naval bases or border crossings.

Public Holidays

Turkey's public holidays are as follows:

January 1	New Year's Day
April 23	National Independence and Children's Day
May 19	Atatürk's Birthday
August 30	Victory Day, for 1922 war with Greeks
October 29	Republic Day

Festival of Ramadan *(Ramazan)*, ninth month in Muslim lunar calendar, is not an official holiday, but observed by the faithful with fasting and prayer. Many shops and bazaars close on the *Şeker Bayramı* (Sugar Festival) at the end of Ramadan and, just over two months later, on *Kurban Bayramı* (Day of Sacrifice).

Public Transport

Long-distance buses from the *otogar* (bus station) are privately owned and highly competitive. Only the more expensive companies offer buses with non-smoking or air-conditioning. Taxis run on the meter, so you should not have to haggle over fares, but write down your destination as the driver rarely speaks other than Turkish. *Dolmuş*, shared taxis, run on specific routes, letting you off for a pre-set fare, much cheaper than by taxi.

Time Difference

Turkey is two hours ahead of GMT and puts the clocks forward an hour in summer.

Tipping

Service is included in hotel and restaurant bills, but you can always add a little extra. Apart from hairdressers or private tour-guides, tipping is much less customary than you might imagine and you should respect polite refusals.

Toilets

Men have fewer problems than women, but if you don't want to "go Turkish", take advantage of facilities at hotels or tourist restaurants. Toilet paper is rarely provided so carry a spare roll in your bag. It should be placed in the basket beside the toilet, not flushed away, for you might block the pipes.

INDEX

Adana 41–42
Aksaray 50
Alanya 37–38
Anamur 39
Andriake 27
Antakya 26, 39, 42
Antalya 29–30
Antiphellos 25
Aspendos 33, 35
Atatürk 52
Avanos 47–48
Caravanserai 35, 50, 52
Çayağzi, see Andriake
Cilician Gates 41
Dalyan 21
Demre 26–27
Derinkuyu 39, 48
Dim Çayı 38
Eğirdir 32, 51
Fethiye 17–19
Gazipaşa 39
Göreme 39, 46
Hatay 42
Ihlara Valley 39, 48–50
Kale, see Demre
Kalkan 23, 32
Kaş 23–25, 26
Kaya 19–20
Kekova 25–26
Kemer 31
Kızkalesi 40–41
Konya 50–51
Letoön 22
Manavgat 35
Myra 27, 39
Nevşehir 44
Ölüdeniz 20–21
Patara 22–23
Perge 32–33
Phaselis 32, 35
Saklıkent 31
Side 33–35
Silifke 39
Sultanhanı 11, 50
Tarsus 41
Telmessos 18
Termessos 30–31, 32
Üçağiz 25
Üçhisar 44
Ürgüp 47
Uzuncaburç 39–40
Whirling Dervishes 50–51, 53
Xanthos 21–22

Series editor: Barbara Ender-Jones
Design: Luc Malherbe
Photos: front cover, pp. 8, 16, 20, 23, 24, 27, 31, 36, 40, 47 Hans Weber;
p. 49 Bernard Joliat; p. 54 Hémisphères/Frances

Copyright © 1997 by JPM Publications S.A.
12, avenue William-Fraisse, 1006 Lausanne, Switzerland

All rights reserved. No part of this book may be reproduced or transmitted in any form or by any means, electronic or mechanical, including photocopying, recording or by any information storage and retrieval system without permission in writing from the publisher.

Every care has been taken to verify the information in the guide, but the publisher cannot accept responsibility for any errors that may have occurred. If you spot an inaccuracy or a serious omission, please let us know.   Printed in Switzerland.